THE ROSY MEDALLIONS

THE ROSY MEDALLIONS

SELECTED WORK

BY

CAMILLE ROY

KELSEY ST. PRESS

TO REESE ADAMS-ROMAGNOLI

Publication of this book was made possible in part by a grant from the California Arts Council.

PERMISSIONS AND ACKNOWLEDGMENTS

"Missing" first published as "Oct. 8." in *Deep Down: The New Sensual Writing by Women,* © 1989 Faber & Faber. Reprinted as "The Rosy Medallions" in *Women on Women,* © 1990 Plume.

Parts of "My X Story" were published in *The Brooklyn Review 9* under the title "An XY Story," © 1992 Camille Roy.

"BABY" first published in *Mirage #4/Period(ical) #24,* © 1994 Camille Roy.

"Fetish" first published in *Addressing Herself,* a catalog for an exhibition at The LAB (see Notes), © 1994 Camille Roy. Reprinted in *Rooms,* Spring 1994.

LIBRARY OF CONGRESS CATALOGING-IN-PUBLICATION DATA

Roy, Camille
    The Rosy Medallions / Selected Work by Camille Roy.
        p.   cm,
    Contents: My X story — Sex life — Missing — Baby — 2 pure girls — Fetish.
    ISBN 0-932716-35-0
    1. Lesbians — California — San Francisco — Literary collections.
        2. San Francisco (Calif.) — Literary collections.   I. Title.
    PS3568.0945R67   1995
    811'.54 — dc20   95–2637   CIP

BOOK DESIGN

Poulson/Gluck Design

Kelsey St. Press
2718 Ninth Street
Berkeley, CA 94710

Contents

M Y **X** S T O R Y

X and I travel south through a county
> of big white cars
>> & sweet plums—
> there's funk on the radio.
> I wear a low brimmed hat with a feather.

X has on stockings and heels, there's a jaunty cut to her coat.
> She says　　　*With you I felt no guilt.*
>> *I was willing to do almost anything for that.*

Her cigarette makes a red spot in the dark.

I look out at the lights of Bakersfield, Rosedale, Oildale.

The industrial rim marks a boundary

between the city and the desert.　　　*I'm shy about death.*

Before the factories shut down I could see fires

from my window at night.

Car wheels churn gravel up a steep driveway. Ocean, clouds.

I meet Alfred. The ex-husband has a moist tan.

He gives me a room alone

a sky blue window ledge

comfort at being enclosed.

In the afternoon X

presents herself,

looking smart

in a black dress

and little red hat.

I've put on my grey silk tie.

We're compatible in a way,

says X. *I like you, and you*

like my looks.

I have a slip.

White rags

spread with a butter spoon

soft spotting under

my skin —

it's so easy, at first—

my tongue laps her cheekbones

thin as rails

something I lean against while looking out

on a ship,

a tanker,

spidered with helicopters.

Distant line of fire.

Later, we watch one another

as indifferent Alfred smooths the sheets.

When I was small the world started at my stomach
and melted outward in waves. My sisters ate at the same table.
The three boys were farther and measured in their distance,
moving like a clump at sunset along a cord stretched between
two women. One snipped the glowing butt off a firefly and put
it on my finger.

That was Sam. When I was fourteen he did a slide show,
a week after he got his discharge. Pictures of dead people taken
by someone I was related to was the closest I'd ever been to
death. The bodies were lying in tall grass and were hard to see.
Sam had smooth eyebrows over brown eyes and a sloppy jaw,
jerky with amphetamines. He'd enlisted because he loved Gold-
water and when he got out he was a drug addict. But at least he
learned a trade.

Sam was the cousin who leaned down into the window
of the sandwich shop, grinning. He'd landed the helicopter in my
parents' front yard and hitched into town to see me. Around that
time there were rumors he would fly for anyone — running guns
or drugs for the wrong side in small countries. It's not impossible.
Sam worked whenever he wanted, otherwise lived in a trailer
with a woman named Sara.

Composition is like a new car, or kitchenettes.

It creates a frame around disconnected events.

So, after Sara left him for nobody, leaving no note,

Sam wrote a spy novel. That's the story.

For X, sex is a combo of string and

past tense. It covers her yards of mouth.

I lick flesh like an envelope. (Bondage.) Says X,

How bad were you today

baby. Her knees press my temples,

there's a Curly fence near my mouth.

(Imploded recognition.) When I learned

about gender I was very surprised.

The proceedings slid from a folder,

there were loose papers all over the floor.

Before that, I had only

experienced animals. *It's not possible,*

I thought,

Anyone who likes to be fucked is a

girl,

anyone who only likes to be fucked is a

woman.

The soft light over the Los Angeles hills seemed rubbed with an
eraser. I was 16. I felt like I was hitchhiking, since I hardly knew
the cousin who was driving. His name was Jim.

His pickup had beer in the back. We drove up a canyon to his
place, an apartment in a weathered turquoise building next to a
stand of eucalyptus. It was June, and the eucalyptus

had dropped dry skinny leaves all over the parking lot. We walked
up the stairs; inside were Sam, Mike, my sisters. Jim's apartment
was a one-bedroom with a kitchenette.

Mike pulled open the back door to show me what a fucked place
it was: the back stairs had been torn down so the door opened on
empty space. Mike was the family golden boy,

he turned in the light like a fish, sluggish. He left the door open
and settled back on the couch, next to Sam, who drew his long
legs up. It was twilight and through the open door

the sky was turning a deep blue streaked with smoke. There was
an odor of beer. Then the cousins made a show of picking up and
flipping through some porn magazines.

My sisters went for it, arguing like their own sincerity was forever.
It was hard to take. My grandmother was new in the dirt, buried
that day and no one could shut up (except me).

My sister said I shouldn't have sex until my nipples turned brown,
which I figured she thought would never happen. She was older,
and kept her drugs and screwing

in the basement the same way she kept her jewelry there. Her
lovers were thin white men whose trouble was drug-related.
When Paul got out of Cook County Jail he carried an odor of rape

he had large nerve spots in his eyes. Fear moving like a breeze
in a prison yard, I could feel that in my stomach when he was
around; otherwise I didn't care. I thought about Monica.

Her sharp teeth and brown cheeks. The way her greed
slid across my hips could be scary but her palms were
narrow as slots, that made it okay to have sex with her.

Monica was black in a segregated city; so the closer we got

the more transparent I became, my longing vicious as wavering lights of

association. Relation — the spot where we're the same, or at least rolling

downhill on a boulevard lined with palm trees and novelty shops.

So when Sam said *Any real man would rape a 14-year-old*

if he saw her naked,

it shut me up.

Pressure doesn't yield a true statement but softens underfoot,

like nylons in a wad. It's more than gymnastics.

Doors and windows of the body squeak, light as paper.

This carpet I'm eyeing glints back

an acrylic mat, fishy browns.

Next on my list

Thrusting

my hand through

the ribs of X

Warm slimy blood

on my fingers,

bits of bone

What a mess.

I want to do

something

for you,

I say

to X, staring

at my hand.

I wrap it

in my shirttail;

now it looks like a bandage

though the gesture

was sexy & fun.

One day after school Monica brought me home.

I sat on a yellow chair and we listened to the radio: *WVON,
Otis Spann The Blues Man,* coming from the kitchen. A plaid
couch was covered with sisters with white teeth and dark
skin, laughing at me I thought. The rooms were hot, or just full
of the weather and leaning out over the window sills I saw
white stone pots of geraniums at the door. We watched the
street — a tall drunk wobbled after a woman in a flowered
house dress whose crooked eyes bulged out in two direc-
tions. She turned and hacked out a laugh. Monica said her
stomach split every year with a new kid.

<u>Or was that my block?</u>

*I liked the closed-in feeling — relation defined through position and
abandonment, the meaning of* **fix***. So the streets were deserted after
dark and any stranger carried death!*

It's one a.m., and the snow is falling
through a web of fine black particles, soot from the mills.
Monica's shielding her cigarette from the wind while I try to
remember where I am; on a block that slides uneasily from
white to black. She's wearing a red T-shirt under her black
jacket. We've just come out of the basement. We started
out watching each other, lips back, drinking beer. Where
our skin slides together along the damp basement wall,
there's a streak of feeling like a welt. I open another beer,
to sink this awful strangeness. Then her palms are warm
and under my jaw, sliding back around my head. That's
okay, so I peel off her T-shirt, it is very interesting how dark
her nipples are. I touch them with my fingers then my lips
then I lean back, feeling thin as a sheet. I'm washed out,
ripped. She kisses me clear to the back of the throat,
where the tongue splits. I figure I don't

She tells me her mama said *You're old enough
to know to keep your pocketbook closed,* and we laugh about that.

Monica walks into school
her fingers loosely rolled
a snap to her stride.
It's September.
Still summer
there's that other kind of light.
Weeds line the cracks, there are gardens in vacant lots.

Between classes we're kept in formation, thin lines of skittish kids on opposite sides of the hall. Green iron bars cover the windows. Gang wars edge in over the grey pavement of the school yard. Monica is light on her feet, quick by necessity. I want to please — I don't know why — I follow and give her books from the library. *I'm sorry they're stolen,* I say. She says, *Sorry didn't do it, you did,* and laughs. Like she does when she tells me about the death. Even I know that's wrong, to laugh at her daddy, dragged out of his taxicab, dead of a heart attack at 44. It's late in the day. We're standing by the window in an empty classroom, the sky behind her shoulder is a dull blue. When I tell her to quit laughing, she wipes a smile on and runs out of the building.

She got poorer after that. She had to move out of the district.

X spreads gleaming

micas across her eyelids

& clips her hair. The

blond ends fall on a

glass-topped vanity table.

Her relatives cut their

hair off before they split

up

               she's heard that. She strokes her lips
               red. *I'm the private glamour in a dead*
               public, she thinks. After each orgasm
               she's happy for hours, it makes her want
               to change course and slip

under what she wanted before. Pursing her lips for the mirror,
I should hang cool sight lines next to the bed, a thin frame
containing light footsteps across water. If I were certain of
finding what I want, she wonders, *would I become smaller.*

X and I are driving through a warehouse district after getting out of a movie. I'm morose; my mood is bruised. X stubs out her Camel filter and asks *What's the matter, babe. Too much wild, wild life?*

I'm thinking about the moment when Freddie Kruger jumped out of thin air. *Horror movies seem so familiar,* I say. *It's like waiting grimly for some lunatic thing to pop out of a family member's mouth; then it happens and you want to slide under the table. But I like to go to them; they're so repetitious. It's like my own private joke.*

X says **You feel vindicated when something horrible happens.**

I'm thinking it's true, it's the only thing that makes the inexplicable burst like a bubble. I look out the window at the warehouses.

Nah, I say, finally. *It's just that something always pops out that reveals the essential nature. And you're either waiting for it, or you've been set up, and which is better.*

X laughs, sort of cautiously.

It's that climate of expectation, I say. *Like when I was a kid and it would get so fucking hot even the Lake* was hot but you had to go swimming

even though the Lake had pee in it.

I mean a lot of pee

and dead fish. It was that hot.

I was with my sister

before she was a beatnik

she was wearing a yellow bathing suit

with a white belt and cat eye glasses.

She was sitting on the beach

eating a hot dog with pickle relish

and reading her theatrical magazines.

I ran in diving and splashing

coming up inside a bunch

of grinning kids whose teeth gleamed

like an ad for toothpaste.

The biggest pushed my head under

once, twice. I surfaced gasping

knees scraped.

The horizontals were dazzling

those stacked grins like ladder rungs

I couldn't climb.

A glimpse of a withered grey pier

then a black finger in my eye

and the shining water smacked my chin.

I was under again.

I started to kick.

I must've made some noise

because my sister ran into the water,

waving her hot dog.
My tormentors scattered at the sight
of her adult-size thighs, laughing.
That was it.

I'd thought skin color was decorative.

I found out it was territorial.

And I stayed out of the water, walking up and down the beach
picking up pieces of worn bottle glass, mostly green some red
and blue. Blue was the rarest.

X says, *You mark time backwards to the moment of damage.*

She threatens but she won't leave me. I'm already missing something.
If there's a window in the room I'm looking out of it, leaning against
the wall, hands stuffed into my pockets. I frown a lot, my face has
acne scars.

        Now Christmas eve is on with
strings of big colored bulbs in the living room,
and Eartha Kitt is drawling *Santa, baby....* on
the radio. I pick up the 'Sporting News' while X
finishes her dressing, fastening a brooch with red
and green paste jewels to her wool crepe jacket,
then pulling on little Xmas boots, spike white
heels under red felt. I have a weird yearning to get
fucked up. Lately my mind sort of plops from one
to the other of all the drugs I've got in the house.
I've got heroin in the basement, I think, while
reading about the baseball contracts.

X likes hallucinogens and I like opiates — one of our differences.

X's chopped hair is cut like a cap.

She leans towards the mirror

gently pulls one lower eyelid down

then draws the short stub

under her lashes, making a thin black line.

When done with both eyes

she tosses the pencil into the trash.

Another girlfriend gone.

X gave me the word this morning, but
I can't think about it.

*…those perfect pouty lips…It was really a bad sign when
she painted them red before 9:30 in the morning…*

I stare at those lips. An impossible disruption. Breach, that's
what this is. My mind foams, *Am I on the other side?*

It's my way or the highway, babe, says X.

An elastic grin surfaces under my feet. If we could
just shut up when we get close to one another —
then I'd be action NO PLOT, while X marks
the beginning of the story. I eroticize dread.
It's beginning again. Is our aggression a manner of speaking,
conversation taking shape?

More wishes:
A white car or a wide receiver.

Driving in the narrative of shadow.

X tells me I'm too much for her aching stomach.

I say, *If I left you I could steal anything.*

Afternoon sun flattens the beige shingles of the apartment building where I used to live. There's something unexpectedly cool about the reflected yellow light. In one window a FOR RENT sign hangs. That apartment has two radiators in it, I happen to remember. My taste for accuracy is like gleaming chrome window knobs on an abandoned car. The apartment is roomy, there's room for two. X worked as a bookkeeper and I was a thief. Once I stole a whole Xerox machine and stripped it for parts. It was there when Camille, a neighbor, bought a stereo and speakers from me for 75 bucks. X gave her attitude, eyeing her disdainfully while painting her toenails on the couch. I think Camille liked that. She's the kind that likes a bruise. Anyhow she seemed pretty interested when she was casing our stuff. There's not much of a market for hot copiers. I piled what I couldn't sell in the middle of the living-room floor when we left town.

I knew those two. Frank, the building manager, told me they left an answering machine behind when they split, with a bunch of messages on it from *your husband Alfred.* Frank ran into them when they were packing up their car, a white '67 Plymouth Valiant with decorative turn signals on the hood and a dark red interior. They said they'd be going south down Interstate 5 to Bakersfield, then cutting east to Las Vegas. He was surprised that they were all paid up on their rent, but I wasn't. It was the honest bookkeeper girlfriend, settling accounts. She had the soft round eyes of a calf and a smudged pout. When I bought a stereo from them she eyed me like I was one of her girlfriend's vices. I figure the thief was the kind who ignored bills. She had long skinny thighs and a weird bob in her walk, like her joints were too loose. She was secretive but could flash a warm smile on and off, at least for me.

That got me razzed; I don't know why. I want to peel that smile off and put it in my pocket.

S E X L I F E

It was an August day, hot and clear. I stuck out my thumb as cars zipped by. After they passed I started walking down the tarmac road, through a county of red dirt and warped tiny pines. I was going to work. Eventually a dusty hatchback skidded to a halt at the shoulder. When I opened the door there was a shiny revolver on the passenger seat. The driver said *I'm an off-duty policeman,* flashed a big goofy grin and stuck the gun into the glove compartment. That's the way it started. I remember there was a light at the end but no tunnel.

Bright blue sky reflected in gun metal.

My sex life begins later, in a tiny loft above Sam's Health Foods Store. The whites of Sam's eyes were yellow as scrambled eggs, and his wiry hairs seemed about to spring off his head. Sam employed me and Max, his brother. Although Max was only 22, he had a musty old man smell and hair grew out of his ears. Sam let me sleep in the store's loft when I worked till closing. After I wiped the counters and dropped the day's wad of cash in the bank slot across the street, I'd climb the ladder up to Max's pile of porn.

Why are there so many body parts?, I wondered as I fingered Max's magazines. The only body in that hot crawl space was mine. I gently touched the women's cunts, scalded pink cracks. On these nights my mind rose out of my body and floated around the rafters, dry as dust. It's that sexual specificity, like rocks in the brain. Do you know what I mean? I was 18 and it was stunning. Fantasies lurched through my mind like drugs. Any feeling was appropriate because my head was empty. I started carrying a knife when I hitched rides to work. I'd sit in the back of the car and imagine playing their throats like violins. *After I'm done with you, confession will be a relief.* Lots of guys had pony tails then, which made it easier.

Twinkle little star, give me your revolver — that's what I said to the off-duty policeman as I opened the glove compartment. I giggled when he threw me out.

There was a dyke story in one of Max's porn magazines. It was my favorite, but not because I liked it exactly. Reading it by the light of my flashlight was like examining a photograph of dead relatives. On the first page there was a drawing of the author, 'Lisa V.', grinning crazily as she rowed a small boat on a stormy ocean. The dizzy feeling of the picture had something to do with eating pussy, which was explained carefully, step by step, to the male audience. The story reminded me of Anita, only because it didn't resemble anything we'd done together.

Anita was a small person and her moans sounded like soft hoots. She cracked out shaky orgasms that left me clutching her fingers. Hers was my first pussy and I enjoyed playing with it. I tried flicking her clit with my finger as I listened to her breathing. But sex with Anita was mild, like a survey. We did this-and-that — whatever she'd spent her marriage fantasizing about. Once I tongued her asshole, because she wanted me to. Then I felt nauseated. "Why'd you make me do that?" I said. She giggled and grabbed my tit. "You'll do whatever I want you to do," she said.

Anita had a husband, Mark, and me (before I left the state), but they kept me a secret. I was 18, and Anita was my first.

What's with the body anyway, I said to Anita, and she said it has to do with space, occupation. *Give it a try,* she said, backing me into a corner.

Put your legs and arms up — expect a circus. Is it possible to walk away if you don't like it anymore? Anita's legs were lights underwater. I stood as still as a butler, I didn't know where I was. The husband Mark replaced me, but not before I'd tasted her cunt.

Mark and Anita picked me up in the cafe where I worked. It was pretty easy I guess. They sat at a table in my section for several hours, swapping stories of payoffs, political vendettas, feuds between the police and fire departments, and I drifted by, listening. I noticed Mark first, actually. He had a cynical way of nibbling at a cigarette. Anita stabbed little pieces of cheese with a toothpick, and drank white wine. When she looked up from her glass she was usually staring at me. It turned out they were newspaper reporters. And they knew a good bar, etcetera.

It was a nearly empty jazz club. Anita danced by herself, spinning around the small dance floor with her arms swaying, while Mark and I leaned against the back wall, watching her.

Mark was neat and compact with dark hair. Anita had small perky tits. Even sitting back on the couch, after we got to their apartment, her nipples pointed up through the soft knit top she was wearing with jeans. Her torso was square atop long slim legs, and she had a big pillow of wavy auburn hair. But her face was distractingly broad, a fat person's face. Mark took a hundred dollar bill out of his wallet, rolled it into a thin tube, and passed it around on a mirror with lines of cocaine.

Coolness at the back of my throat while I tried to fall asleep. Murmuring from Mark and Anita's bedroom, then quiet. Dim street light bled through the curtain over the couch, where I was curled under a pinkish yellow blanket. Every time something happens I adjust to a different kind of silence. Perhaps they had tense words as I was sliding gently out of consciousness, but I heard nothing. I woke with a start to hear Anita's slow sobs, a low throbbing like a cello. Her cries were bleak beyond disclosure, though their door was open a crack. It flooded me with excitement, a sexual disturbance. As it went on and on she began to sound like the rhythm of my breathing, and I fell asleep.

Nothing much happened for the next few weeks. The three of us hung around together and I spent more nights on their couch, while the point (which even I knew was sex) didn't seem to be getting any closer. Not that I cared very much; I wanted experiences. Was I going to turn into a lesbian? Anyhow, I wondered where the sex was — Mark and Anita didn't seem to be having any, at least while I was lying out there. Then, suddenly, they did. I heard every moan, because the door was open a crack, as I sat by the coffee table wiping the mirror clean with my finger and rubbing the leftover cocaine on my gums. Buzz.

Weeks later Anita asked me what I thought. I didn't know what she was talking about. *Just tell me your impression.* She was pushy like that. So I told her I was amazed how much noise Mark had made, those moaning noises — it sounded so femme. She laughed at my inexperience. *In the movies men don't make noises like that when they're screwing*, I said.

The next time I spent a night on their couch, Anita began sobbing again. Then she stopped, and Mark came out in his bathrobe. He lit a cigarette and sat down in the chair across from the couch.

"I'm going away for two months," he said, "I understand you are going to fuck my wife." He jabbed his cigarette out in the ashtray and sighed. "Anita's had the hots for you from the start."

Their door was open. I imagined her listening, curled in their bed, eyes open and face wet.

The next time I came around their place Mark was gone. Nothing changed except Anita seduced me and we started doing it all the time. What I mean is that the connection between us didn't intensify. When she wanted sex a glare would lurch out of her, a kind of cold pornographic light. It embarrassed me. Once afterwards she looked at me with an amused expression and asked, *Are you a dyke yet?* I mumbled something and she said, *Well you choose your apples.*

I was her idea, the fix for a wife with lesbian dreams. She never told me the details but I could feel them pushing out at night, in the way that there's a ghost town inside every city. It made her ferocious but not personal. She really thought I'd be grateful later. *Adolescence is a form of brain death,* she told me. *Thanks,* I said, and she laughed. Now she's silent because she's in the past, like someone dead.

Once she wanted me to tell her my sexual fantasies. *Confession is good information*, she said, stroking my clit with her finger. I shuddered, then recoiled. What could I say? My mouth was unconscious. I should have whispered, *It feels like your nostalgia.*

Anita was supposed to make me a dyke; that's what I was waiting for. It sounds so stupid, she put out in almost every manner I could want. But I felt I was sticking around because I didn't get it yet — was this lesbianism? I had wanted a different surprise; I kept waiting for her to give me one. I wish I could say I got fed up and left. But Anita actually told me it was time, once Mark got back. I don't remember exactly what she said, but it was something along the lines of *Don't you have better things to do, now that you're all grown up.*

Anita hated writing journalism. She really thought of herself as a poet. Once, after reading her own article in the newspaper, she said, *You can't pummel vivid into a normal sentence. It's hopeless as marriage.* So I wrote her a note before I left. "Thanks for everything," it said, and then I tacked on a quote she'd found in some magazine. It was Gary Gilmore, interviewed by Norman Mailer. "You want to learn how to be an artist? Then learn how to eat pussy. That's the only art you'll ever need to learn."

It's scenic around here. People come to bathe in the desert springs. Red rock cliffs splinter like icebergs. Outside the store, a forest of piñon pines grows as high as my knees, and the dust is a fine red sand. Sam's customers are mostly tourists, they sit at the tables outside with their bags of carrot chips and herbal ice tea. The breeze smells like sage. I rinse the sponge and wipe the counter, then take a bite of organic cream cheese coconut cookie. It's tender as clouds.

I'm still working my way through Max's porn. I wonder if he knows. Nasty Max — he makes cracks about my hitchhiking. *Then drive me to work,* I say. I call him Trash Can behind his back, because of the junk he eats. Max says, if I don't watch my ass, the local psycho killer will pick me up. *Who might that be,* I ask, and he snickers.

Sex life, sex death — I don't have an opinion. I've got a waist and a knife instead. Anita said the difference between a violent act and a sexual one was that if you chopped all the fantasy out of the violence there'd be something left over: *damage.* But sex without fantasy — is nothing. When I read Max's porn, I like to think of that particular nothing and what falls into it. That reminds me of my life.

The day I first saw her was a day the fog didn't clear. Whiteness smothered everything, a kind of extinction. I'd been spending my days off wandering aimlessly, and that day I'd gone to the park, stopping on a footbridge to watch the ducks. A dank little lake filled the bottom of a ravine and there were very few ducks. It seemed hard to move or think; maybe I was hungry. I was staring at the oily water when someone appeared, walking towards me through the tangled groves of eucalyptus. She drew near and then stopped, leaning over the railing next to me. I shifted my gaze to her feet — men's shoes, narrow, with the thin creases of expensive leather. Cuffed pants. Her dark grey gabardine coat was cut generously, well below the knee, and belted like a trench coat. I turned towards her but the stranger was oblivious, her dark blue eyes looking down at the water. Everyone has her own private thoughts, but her disdain was striking. It was as obvious as the creases in her skin and the steely grey of her closely cropped hair. This was a pervert, remote as a vampire who has aged. Shock settled into my shoes; I had never seen anyone like her before. A pervert with money. The thought made my teeth hurt, but filled me with modesty. I wanted to dance about in a white embroidered gown, to show how dreamy I was; it was the only quality of mine I could think of which might be attractive to her. The inadequacy of this idea rattled me, and I was staring at the water with a twisted expression when she spoke.

"The poor dog has arthritis. This damp weather doesn't agree with him."

There was a small white poodle at her feet.

"What happened to him?" I asked. He had three legs and a grim expression.

"Claude had an accident with a bear trap."

Nothing about her encouraged questions, and as I looked at the maimed poodle I felt caution slow my breathing. It was oddly pleasurable, to stand next to her and notice my own apprehension.

"How far do you think the dollar will fall?" she said eventually, in a soft voice.

"Has it fallen?"

"It's lost 25% of its value against the yen. And about 13% against the deutsche mark."

"Oh," I said, jumping on a feeling of rich disdain, "capitalism goes on binge and purge cycles. You can't stop it."

"Yes. Things have gotten out of hand," she said with interest.

"The profit motive!" I said dismissively. When she didn't respond I added, "What can you expect but slime and corruption!" I felt so sure of myself I spoke ridiculously, and laughed out loud. She was quiet for so long I was afraid our conversation had ended. I felt ashamed for using the word 'slime.' Finally, she turned to me with a quizzical expression.

"Currency speculation is a dangerous game. I myself recently averted disaster — in ways I should be ashamed of. But I find it impossible to re-member why, exactly, I did all of this. Any of it."

I knew you would never be wholehearted. I recognized your sly face as soon as it appeared, making light of my disappointments. Your witty eva-siveness likewise, and then your boredom. With anyone else this would have meant no sex, I sense these things from the start. But with you I was impelled, awkward, even grabby, and I feel at fault, though all that happened also seems somehow entirely your fault.

"I followed you. I think you're interesting." At her doorway I suddenly acquired my father's clear enunciation, each syllable a protruding embarrassment. She took my shoulder, gently steered me into the house, and shut the door.

"I noticed you."

I followed her through a dark hall, though the rooms on either side seemed full of light. It led to a library, comfortably outfitted with built-in bookcases and a velvet couch with deep cushions. All the colors were rich and dark, while outside the windows a willow stirred in a breeze, making a panel of rippling green. She seemed clear and unworried, picking up a few things, laying her coat over a chair. Her disdainful expression had shifted to amusement. That's what I am, the amusement, I thought, and felt tired. I hoped I wouldn't have to do most of the talking, and sat down cautiously on the couch.

"You caught us by surprise." This in a wry, but friendly, tone.

Writing this, there's a sharp sense of visibility decreasing. The literalness of my desire feels disjointed, slides off from the target. All this breath between myself and what I remember — a body and its pleasures. You invited me in. The shock of that disconnects me.

She stopped and looked at me with misgiving, as if registering my presence for the first time. "Why are you here?"

"I don't know, you asked me." It's too late, I thought, you can't kick me out. The weary sliding away of her eyes made me pushy — I lit a cigarette and put my feet on her coffee table.

She shook her head irritably. "Sorry. I get annoyed when I don't know what I'm doing."

I could stay. Relieved, I sank back into the cushions and surveyed the room. There was a black table with swollen claw feet, and something shiny above me, a brass chandelier. My neck is a lure, I thought, laid out on her brown velvet cushions. I felt its muscles contract as I slowly said, "I like it here." Then I took a long drag on my cigarette.

She smiled sideways, a sharp smile not directed at me. "You're ridiculously young." She swung around to the chair next to the couch, sat down, leaned forward, and nudged my leg with her finger.

"So what's your name?" she asked.

"Patty Hearst."

She laughed with a gratifying hard burst. "Would Patty like a drink?"

"A whiskey sour please," I mumbled, feeling drunk already. But she didn't have sour mix, just whiskey straight up, which was soon swirling in the bottom of my glass. Whiskey reminds me of my mom. For some reason this struck me as really funny and I smiled foolishly at her.

One thing I like is she makes me feel I don't need to know much. It's a relief not to have to understand your own experiences. The room was warm, the books seemed packed and secure in their built-in bookcases. Suddenly I wanted to talk for a long time, or else be very quiet on that soft brown couch, leaning back and studying the layer of whiskey in my glass.

Lifting my hair off my neck as if it were very heavy, she gently touched my neck with her lips, then her teeth. Then she leaned against the back of the couch, swirling the ice in her glass with her finger. Her eyes had that hot look adults get when their routines are busted and anything could happen.

"How you doing? You ever done anything like this before?"

Have I ever — that's funny, I thought. I bared my teeth and a weak smile turned into "Yes." I sounded like a liar.

She shrugged and traced the outline of my lips with her finger, ran her hand down my throat. "Nice skin," she said.

Leaning back, she draped her hand across her lap. That shift on her face I thought must be a smile, perhaps an ironic one. A sexual flare had followed her hand across my face. I wanted to cover myself. I thought of striking her, the interesting sparks off that hard, long life.

"Anything special I should know about?" she asked me.

"No, of course not."

It was a good time to get up and walk around the couch, to get myself between her legs. But I seemed to move slowly, I couldn't get used to the speed.

"No of course not," she said gently, mocking me. Hand on my shoulder, the slow approach was beginning to make me suffer. "We'll see."

Her mountainous perversity is like buckets of hair. Buckets of finally hair, at a time of night when I get my pronouns confused. It's the kind of image or scene you want to describe to your friends but it's so weird that no openings come up in regular conversation.

____

Her hand on my shoulder, that first gesture of invitation, was characteristic of her. Circular as a huge conscience, something to follow indefinitely. Her fingered good-byes marked my body. Even this story, its thin crust, marks her evasions.

So the room was either dark or light, or was two rooms. There were implements beyond my consciousness. Sharp cravings make narratives, also subjects. So it was easy to let her carve it, warble wobble. Only by turning on her with all my teeth bared could I regain ground already lost. Of course I did it. Of course yearning made it impossible. Pleasures of the rupture, rack and screw.

All over her, squall. Green wet rose, puff of smoke.

She had a collection of crops framed under glass. Each one had a name under it: Lady Fastbuck, Mary Mountbatten. She said these were mementos of the days when she rode in steeplechases. "It is hard to do this," she said, kneading my breast in the rhythm of her breath.

My moment in the hallway: I want to sit on the French inlaid bureau under the crops and get fisted. Marks rise to the surface of my neck. When did she put on that leather jacket; it's causing long prickly emotions down my back. Pulling at her shirt I attack the decency of white cotton, attaching myself via red lines I draw in her flesh. She's rubbing her crotch. "Let me see your tits," she says.

I drop my shirt for her, push my breasts together hard enough to feel their resistance. Then I slide out of my jeans, my shoes. Dropping item by item on the rug, I'm oddly comfortable with my body. There's a curious sense of touching the thick carpet only with my heels, perfect rounds of skin.

She pushes me towards the next room. Her bedroom — a place for my shiny and submissive death — I'm reluctant. If I'm going to abandon the real world, the one made up solely of dressed people, I want her to, also.

I want to say *shut up* though she is silent. Instead I twist out of her grasp & lean against the window. The glass is cool against my cheek and hardening nipples, then below there's a grassy sloping garden and the willow. Her hands are on my hipbones, they slide down slow & firm as if following a groove. "Slow down," I say. "No," she says, her voice calm and flat. "I'll slow down later." Then she laughs, and her teeth graze my neck. My breath fogs the glass. "Please baby," I say. "What?" I twist around to look at her face. There's a slight smile but her eyes are wide with desire. I slip my arm beneath her shirt and run my lips along her jaw line. "Fist me," I whisper and what slides up my cunt and unfolds is a smooth genital pain.

Then her hand disappears in my fur and I tighten my thighs around her leg to grasp it. Sliding down, riding her knuckles, the juices of my cunt, her expensive pants. Hand on my shoulder, she looks down at the wet mark and laughs. I suddenly like her; this new affection streaks through my body like aggression. I undo her pants and push them down; her clit is warm and wet under my tongue. She slides down the wall into a heap, leans her head to one side. "What do you think you're doing?" she asks quizzically.

"Making advances," I say. She leaps forward and we're rolling on the floor like dogs. What orders the flow is aggression — hers. Maybe she's not really a sadist. Possession is the deepest, thickest point. I could work that, and draw out desire even when she's not interested. I twist over, guilty. But she's grasping my buttocks with both hands. Bent over the edge, a lattice of hands, her rosy palms smacking my tin flesh.

I'm getting rosier and rosier. There's no telling where we are. These large sensations come and go. I want to be a star. I want to be adorable. Instead there are the larger sensations, so open there is a sense of leveling. What is inside slips out and vanishes. So when I am finally on my back again and she fists me with her total possessiveness, I am wholly (not) there having left (come), fucked to heaven.

There it is, the house on the corner. It's brown with darker window frames, curled up like a fist. But not aggressive — it seems to be holding something; the house looks thoughtful. You wouldn't know from outside how light streaks in through the library windows, through the many small square panes that face the park, and the row of cypresses growing there. They're grim trees, I think. It's an especially clear light because the library is above the street, on the second floor. The Bonnard gives the room a watery sheen. It's a room no one can peer into, a room we pad about in, casual, as if privacy were ordinary.

Presenting myself so bluntly becomes a more or less humiliating mistake depending on the level of your interest. I'd be content to sink into this wordless stomach you run your fingers across, if you only talked to me occasionally. But you treat me like I'm young. That's one of your miscalculations, hovering among the gleam of appliances and brass. It wears thin, like the kitchen, this table also, and your blush after three drinks.

My argument is simple: your face is a place to sleep.

Days pass in your kitchen, you make soup, a sourish chicken soup with gelatinous noodles, or a beef barley with wine and rosemary. You boil whole tiny red potatoes, we eat them with butter. You are tender, rub my shoulders, lightly season the trout before sautéing.

Today I want to move into the small dark room in the back of the house —
it's a maid's room probably. I'll do it when you go grocery shopping. Now
you're watching football. Here the phone never rings, no paper arrives.
You live in the half-light of some shrewd investments, and tell me I'm
young — I should live in Paris! That's a hint, of course. The maid's room
sits in the back of my mind. With a few arrangements, it's a place I could
vanish in.

These notes were handwritten on 3-holed notebook paper. I found them
under her bed. She was my roommate; we worked at the cafe together.
After she disappeared I waited a few days, but then I couldn't stand it
anymore and I went through everything in her room — not that there was
much — jeans, shirts, some political pamphlets. She was the kind of per-
son who would resent me calling the police more than anything, whatever
had happened. Perhaps these pages explain where she went. I've pre-
served their order. Some were deliberately torn across the bottom, and I
couldn't find the missing parts. These tears seemed possibly meaningful
so I have marked their location.

BABY
OR
WHOSE BODY IS MISSING?

BABY can't stop himself from being born. Cut from a knotted uterus then jerked free, he's so sick he can't breathe. BABY's grey as a rat & limp as a noodle. Rivulets of blood run through his toes & puddle on the blue sheet covering his entire mom. The doctor and nurses are wearing blue sheets, with white latex fingers poking out. Metal implements hang from the white walls. The doctor lifts BABY up before the witnesses and says,

People are looking for solutions however reluctantly, because drugs are unfashionable.

BABY looks down on his large flowing blue mom. He cannot see anything of her body but a red slit and blood sliding across the blue folds.

Someone takes hold of BABY, lays him on a metal shelf, and puts a plastic bubble over his mouth. BABY begins to breathe oxygen smoke as he looks up at the blue masks of his doctors. BABY's eyes are hazy. But it's not a result of wanting money or drugs. Before BABY learns how to think, he has a thin grammar.

Meanwhile, conversation passes like plates among the white asses of the doctors. No one is listening to BABY, who says,

I feel I'm just the logical result of certain families breeding with each other. History has something to do with it, but not as much as you think.

■

BABY will never remember his first breath.

He won't remember his body arriving, either.

■

All objects ARE frustration (is a theory about art). The body is
plumbing and consciousness, so you feel your toast before you taste it.
Pain folds a person's cranium.

I'll explain circumstances to all you minors.
- i)   The picture is big,
- ii)   The picture rains on us,
- iii) I'm coated with picture.

Understanding requires free time, and no one's time is free.
(Restless stratification.)

Here is a picture of BABY:
His skin is soft as butter.
His eyelashes peek like little lambs then curl up.
He is quiet as a pocket.

Mom is dripping, little puddles of white form in her nipples
and the whole house smells of milk. Mom's understanding is perfect.
She knows that the nipple is the only object that ISN'T frustration,
so she puts her nipple in BABY's mouth.

Mom says, I'm so glad the BODY arrived (kiss kiss).

BABY is sucking. Then BABY lifts his head & says,
"I'm the only one whose body isn't missing."

■

I was a bar dyke before all this gender-theory crap came along. I kissed
and fucked like every other girl in my invisible world, and I stuck dollar
bills in the g-strings of all the strippers in town. That world is still invisible,
because I left my body there.

*If you believe that, find the burial at the end of this sentence.
Do you know whose body is waiting for you there?*

No one can see anything before I get dressed. After I get
dressed, I am a sex toy. This happened even before I became a lesbian,
or a mother, or a girl. It is a very personal, very feminine thing: minimal-
ism.

It's simple. There's less private and MORE PUBLIC in everyone's life.
How can you see yourself, when you can't even see your information? Is
it local, or does it start in Los Angeles and expand outward like an orgy?

If you think you look like yourself, look for the hole you make in air.
That's what I wanted, when I began these sentences. Now I'm afraid of
poisoning.

■

I see BABY's grammar brain spreading from his big blue eyes across his
face. I'm waiting for tips of intelligence. Recognition begins somewhere,
maybe in language, before any mass starvation. Maybe recognition is
moistened by visuals.

When I talk to BABY I'm talking to the future, with the perfect
understanding only a MOTHER can have. I know for example, that to
restore theatricality to language (that modernism tried to destroy),
BABY'll write a script for a horror movie starring the little wonder slut
of Hollywood, Drew Barrymore.

Which objects are the most scary? Think very delicately,
then put those words into Drew Barrymore's mouth. BABY's tiny pink
lips are the beginning of language, but when he reaches for her nipple,
Drew Barrymore screams. There's a gulf between milk squirting into
BABY's mouth and a moving picture. Why are objects frustrating?
Here's something to try in the privacy of your own home: compare
the neck and lips of a Hollywood slut to the neck and lips of a mule.

BABY doesn't know the difference between mother and
monster. He doesn't know that purses hide money. He can't tell why.

Today June woke me up with one of her creepy dreams:
A man fucked me and my spine burned up.   *It's not a bruise,*
she explains.   She shows me her forehead
the man left his fingerprints there   (dents).

June complains, *I lay down too easily in my little box.*
She kicks off the sheet, picks up a towel, pads into the bathroom.
June's out of brains but she's a love.   We belong together, words
springing from dirt & grievance.   Sisters.

June hums & flushes while I feed my rats (one carrot and a quarter cup
sunflower seeds).   They were miracle births:
                         twins who sat in my womb
                         drank my uterus up, dropped out.
At least they're smaller than I am.

I'm Claire. I got this job. I rake & clip

executive hair. Up at 6

the early train gets me past tight south side streets

to greenbelted new towns in the corn

work in the suburbs.

(Well it's a living.)

I made that up.

June & I pass time

going to school

scraping & creeping around.

I have a movie in my head. I'm spying on it.

Downtown is gloomy but the flats glisten with hysterical sweat

Chicago is yellow

new lights for crimes

yellow bulbs spouting notes.

The cops become bigger

swelling into grey sky they lift off   jerk off

as tour buses pull up next to museums in the sperm rain.

In my movie witnesses are the plot:

sky, city, water, one swallows another

as witnesses hang from trees or gather firewood.

Two kids press their hands together

It is a mistake

June & I are brides of utter definition.

This school was built for a white district:
        front steps a hundred feet wide, roman columns
That was then.

We amble into toothy halls.
June's teacher is swollen. She moves her arms as June
dreams

        I roll over and my color falls off. Rocks enter
        windows, wintry movements through a room.

June makes friends with Deniece after turning over
tables in the cafeteria.   Deniece says,
        Chicago public school system

& June laughs. They kicked her
        Out of greenish halls &
into the street twice last week.

        June says, *So what.*
I'm self-educated.
She whistles, makes a stir,

slicing through
        homeroom with Deniece.
June's hauled off

        to the principal but out by noon.
We eat our lunch as usual
with Averages. Deniece

is an Average, munching
cheese corn from her lunch
bag

but mostly blacks
        clot at the bottom & whites are
XXcelerated. Hyde Park High tracks

        by color. So I'm
a grubby pink ticket
Good for the white part.

Jokes
moisten it but the rocks
        are muddy when

they hit your head.
Walk uneasily. One block after
another slides color —

Don't make a mistake or be sorry
swoon. You can go where
        you can. *Smack, nigger.*

A gun pointed at Jeff's balls. *Honky.*
Someone's rifle barrel slid over Jeff's shoulder as he sat in a car
        smoking a joint.

He whispers about it over lunch,
Poor Jeff, he wants his patch of neighborhood to be hospitable.
        More like a hospital, June says.

Jeff tells us there's trouble in South Shore
        a mob raising fists
over narrow ethnic graves.

Wanna go look?
    Sure

We hop a Stony Island bus & get off when we see the crowd.
A realtor is working the fringes.
        He's brought one black

woman wearing a grass skirt & bones
in her ears, trailing six
scared kids.

He shoves flyers
as he talks to the white noise.   He wants to sell their
        houses.

Drowning in a sea of love, says June.

So when speech dawns like the one world we run like rats
        through the neighborhood
beating pavement through drifts of pale youths.
        It's darker in the avenues
where classmates with O's for mouths chase
        bullets. One for
your pocket, another for your sister.
        That's a gang
built from thousands of fibers.

It's spring.

The lake opens like a purse and dead fish
        spill out onto the beaches.
The west side burns. There's a shooting
        then a big storm.
Out in the alley we play thunder
        with rolled socks.
It's a dead end, a sweet half circle with white curbs.
        We punch one another and leap
shrieking into the rain.

June's suspended for a week   says the principal.
Don't go out   bubbles from mom's coral mouth
floating in smoke.   So June waits by the window
open grinding
wind   & soft
tangled curtain.   She takes off her earrings & watches the dry trees.

When Jack comes through the back gate
June tears off her face,
slides on fishnets.
Jack doesn't notice.
He sits on the sticky plastic couch
nibbles her mouth
swallows
then Jack's grey eyes wobble up
from June's
red lips.
Suck her face, I say.
Go away,
June snaps.
Poor Jack.
Bad breath & black skinny trousers.
Mom chases him
with the cranberry Fuller Brush air freshener.
Jack's a junior. I'm younger
skinny too
leaping around the couch.
Think speedy, I yell at Jack,
Speedy waits for no one.
But Jack's feeling down
chewing his lip.
Jack's mouth interests me.
Last week a tooth dropped out
now he fiddles with the lip flap.
There's scabs on his arm.
Foggy Jack—he lasts
a couple months
after that. June cries
when he dies.
Her hair flies up
in wasps' nests,
tears jerk out.
Mom mom mom, she says
& cool fingers float over June's soft hair.
Mom likes us, I tell her.
But June moves out.

CALL JUNE, mom snaps
Find out how she is.
But I know she's asleep   her blanket twisted
over her stomach
grey
lips mumbling

     June dreams the dying elms wave and walk under a blue sky
     The sun is planted in dirt so the soil trembles with light

Mom cries. June dies
like the oranges
with a great
smell
I made that up
    I have a new habit
       pure as love
         I follow
           my fingers down
             rub across wiry
              hairs
                pull the sheet up
                  between my dim legs
                   leaving spots
cute
bloody.

Reaching
down in the dark
between my legs
I found two rats
I call them
Samuel
& Emmanuel.

June keeps them in her bathtub sprinkling seeds over pink noses and
black fur as she brushes her teeth.

So one day June stops by, chattering about the new boy she likes

NICK — *smart, sells acid.* Her rough voice jumps into a squeal.

When I laugh my mouth turns upside down   it's awful

my brain is a circus of little seeds.

We hear a crash

stumble to the window.

Shots are fired.

A silky figure

walks away.

Only

walking.

Whose dream am I in?

Pow Pow BANG

Let's kill it,

I tell June.

Kill what? she

wants to know.

So how do you like my place?

Fine. I head for the window, picking my way through corn chips and
June's stolen bikinis. The room smells of pot.

June says, *I'm never going home.*

I lean out the window. The air is soft as warm cream. *Just call mom.*

She's crazy, June says.

You're crazy.

Along a thread of yellow sand the lake curves southeast, at the far edge I
can see the World's Biggest Steel Mill. Polacks & blacks worked there.
Now it's closed.

Mom keeps asking me — What is she doing?? I *tell her you're okay,
you're in school, blah blah blah.*

June glares. I go into the bathroom. Not to pee   but to sit on the toilet
and stare at my rats.   Emmanuel is squeaking his tiny
claws slip   claw   slip   up the slanting side of the bathtub.
Working hard.
I bet he's trying to get out of his stupid story.
He tumbles back into the little shit pills and pieces of sawdust
sticks his bubble gum pink nose up in the air. I stroke his spine with my
finger & his bunched haunches tremble under fur.

June comes in.

I saw your rats fucking, she says. *The dick looked like a long pink cord.*

I sprinkle some sunflower seeds in front of Emmanuel.

Deniece invited me to a party, she says.

Samuel wakes up and waddles over to Emmanuel. Now they're both munching.

Are you going? I say.

I already went.

To 45th Street?

June nods. That's where Deniece lives. I laugh so hard I slip off the toilet, big relaxing gasps. Bulldozers rolled over that neighborhood before I was born. North of 47th it's crushed. And black 100%.

What are you laughing at?

Do you remember that time we went there for bar-be-que
& that old man yells
YOU HONKIES GET THE FUCK OUT OF THIS NEIGHBORHOOD
& you said, I dunno what cottage my cheese belongs to.

June cracks up into her splayed fingers.

Everyone knows a perfect object is buried in the middle of the city, but no one remembers where the middle is.

Junkyard with pigs and flies.

The baby in my next dream can talk. He opens his rosebud mouth and words tumble out like tiny gorillas. He says, *If there is a body, there is a center, & someone in charge who can be murdered.* At sunset I wrap the baby in red cloth, and he dies. As I cradle him he turns into a perfect doll, even as the red swaddling cloth rots like the edges of a wound.

Now I'm dead. But I can chew the insides of my dreams into milk and have a live moment.

June yells, *So I went to Deniece's party.*

Words are sick, I say silently. *You stick them in & out of the social.*

June says, *Anyways it was a gang party.*

Oh yeah, I say to myself, *language itches my mouth & falls off.*

June's teeth rattle.

I heard a car drive up. Voices. Deniece turned the music off. I felt uneasy. I guess some Blackstone Rangers came. Someone said, Hide the white girl. So I sat with the shoes in the closet for a while oh less than an hour.

Then Deniece gave me fresh water for two lips & no one stared.

A sunny day. We walk along a path to the beach, dazzled & slapped by tiny waves. Kids are screaming. Downtown skyscrapers form a toothy grin. June nudges me when someone walks up, *This one is an art student, she buys acid from Nick.*

Hi Sally, Nick says.

Sally's blond hair is cut to the jaw, parted on the side & sliding forward over one eye, the other is fixed on Nick. There's a clutch of red lines on her forearm, it's a tattoo of a baby. Sally grins like she's got a mouthful of pretty stones.

SALLY:
My apartment just got ROBBED. They took my stereo
but at least they left the paint brushes. Is there anywhere
we could all go? Anywhere with a little peace...

The rims of Sally's eyes are pink. I say to myself, *Nothing is perfect but
you're insane.*

SALLY:
I've never been robbed before.

I stumble over a blue plastic bucket. Stooping to set it right, I look out
past the white handle at the creamy splashing waves and the sky, so
filled with light the color's washed out. Robbed. The word puts a rattle
in my throat. Different than raped. I've never been raped.

SALLY:
I feel so violated.

Her sincerity is pink as geraniums. Crisp.

SALLY:
This kind of thing doesn't happen where I come from.

What happens where you come from, Sally?

SALLY:
NOTHING.

Everybody laughs. I imagine Sally growing in suburban fields, her
blond stringy hair popping up between rows of corn. She grows bigger
& bigger, finally struggling out of her husk and enrolling in art school.

NOTHING going on means I feel afraid — fear is my retrospective.
Fluffy bursts of color, that's a robbery.

Adrenaline gives everything   a yellow ______ sheen

So June is in the front seat of the car talking to the gun in her face. I'm sitting in the back, relaxed, my wrists hanging over the front seat. June never gives them any money, gun or no gun. She doesn't believe in paying attention. It's a way she fastens herself to the ground and advances word by word. *No money,* she says. *No no money.* I squint at the gun, which I can barely see for the huge yellow sky & say, *We're broke.* The gun droops, I think the guy is staring at us.

GUY with GUN:
Okay. But what were you doing, when I walked up?

ME:
Hello?

JUNE:
This is my sister & she was rubbing my sore shoulder.

GUY with GUN:
Huuhhhh.

He walks off.

June, I say, *he thought we were lesbians.* She snickers, says *fuck.*

I explain all this to Nick & June. Either we didn't get shot because he thought we were lesbians. Or the opposite.

June says, *Why do you always have to figure things out?*

Instead of answering I swing at a fly. Violence is punctuation.
It's my sentence. So sliding the pieces together makes sense of my
walk. And trees and boulders glide by as we are walking again.

SALLY:

The suburbs are really crazy. It's just more hidden.

YOU know about it, June says, *You can trot that insanity out like a
4H PIG.* Sally's face looks pure like it was dead. But she's moving her
lips again. It's that world she comes from, where fields grow houses,
rows upon curving rows.

SALLY:

My mom is a drunk who is so fat her ankles seem to
come from another world. And as for my Dad, he made
his money the good old-fashioned American way: with
brains that degenerated as soon as the cash hit the
bank.

June and I look at one another; something is at stake here and we don't
know what. Then Sally jerks around to face us; she's grinning. I snicker
into my fingers. What a relief. Each breath smacks it in deeper: it's an
okay day. A real day. That's what this is.

I'm walking alone under thin streaks of wet sky
Squat red brick lines the black street
A cool day
Smell of drying pavement
Big clouds unroll over the city
That's what I like
Swirls of white
tear into pieces and head for the Lake
Sidewalk cracks sweat grass
I turn down 53rd, pass the laundry and the YMCA
The cars make splashes
when I stop
breathing
It doesn't seem finished
so I breathe again
walk with my watery hands
as the yellow sun closes.

Today June cried.
Her eyes poured blue at the street.
I came home to find her
at mom's kitchen table
squinting
rubbing
her mouth with her fist.
Nick's busted I make out between June's lumpy sobs.
Now he wants to marry June.
Mom scowls, pissed.
Today is getting bigger
& tomorrow
crashes
our jumpy sour future.
Mom tells me to *Get the hell out.*

So I do
One pure girl
running up the stairs
dreaming of Nick's parole
Wide boulevard   Blazing sun   & Nick wearing sunglasses
and a shiny dark suit
June wanders behind, peering into
wrecked cars and abandoned houses:
Husband & wife.
I slam the door to my room & sit on June's bed (empty for nearly a year)
imagine Nick's grey patch of skin in prison
his slim box getting cracked up the ass
WHAT IS REALISM
A fat bureaucrat
overseeing visiting hours
with 2 dry sockets
June's face is a smashed flower
Cook County Jail can only maintain itself in crime
for it is already in crime.
I curl up on June's old bed.
After a long while with no sound I go downstairs
find mom in the kitchen, slicing carrots.
It's settled mom says
without turning around.
They're not getting married
thank god. But June & I will go every day to the trial. Nick'll look good.
And I'll be helping June apply to colleges. Somebody
somewhere's bound
to take her,
she finishes grimly. Puts her knife down.
I open the back door
Okay mom, I say
& walk down the back stairs.
A few stars glimmer in the washed pale blue sky.

Nick pulls up in his car, and June gets out. She says,

When I was a girl, the strongest feeling in me was to go out.

As far out as I could go.

June goes upstairs and takes off her skirt and pulls on her old soft jeans.

When I walk down June's street, it is full of sun and shining on the
head of grass and greasy street. I turn down the alley, walking across the
tilted slabs of pavement to Nick, leaning against his car. He nods in my
direction.

Upstairs, June folds her clothes. If Nick goes to prison, she mutters,
his eyes'll narrow into slits & dry up into his skull.

This is what happens at the trial:

> *Everyone waits at a long table, their mouths shut. Then the
> Judge enters everyone. June's eyes widen like a melted tangled
> pearl. Nick's are twin holes. The Judge's mouth fondles big
> words, puckering like an asshole.*

Now Sally turns down our alley, her fists jammed into her jeans pockets.
Hiya Sally. She's looking for Nick's drugs. Nick folds his arms over his
white shirt buttoned all the way up with dark glasses in his breast pocket.
His gaze sweeps back & forth like dry brushes.

Sally's big grin fondles us.

How'd it go

she asks Nick.

You mean the trial, Nick says & stops.
Yeah stupid, that's what she means. I spin across the pavement:
step on a crack break your mama's back.

I stop at the log dark under the bushes, by the car. Is that it? Leaning down I stick my hand into the dark overhang, & the little bush leaves quiver. Nick and Sally are talking as dry grasses poke up between my whitish fingers.

Tell June I'll be right back,

says Nick. He walks off down the alley, placing one foot neatly in front of the other, his narrow shoulders rolling slightly as they slide along behind.

Sally props her butt against Nick's car. She tilts her head up towards me, her blond hairs rub & glimmer against her jaw.

Words scratch my throat so I start talking.

To Sally.

Did ya hear, June got a letter saying she was accepted to some college in Oregon. But then they sent her another letter: Dear June your school principal called us up to say that you're a troublemaker and not college material. Don't bother coming here.

That's so fucked, says Sally.

Now June comes down the back stairs, her eyes flick over Sally. Like a change of color, suddenly Sally is terrible.

Where the fuck is Nick says June.

I explain about Nick, then twirl away across the pavement.

When I woke up last night, I was nibbling like my rats. My lips hurt. *I get to be youngest* & have many small dreams, one follows another down the stairs.

Dream #1.

A strange woman has a uterus that is a squid, it speaks,
& each syllable floats off down the dark hallway, an orange fish.

Dream #2.

I'm lying on the floor in the dark next to the strange woman.
I can't move because my hands and feet are at the ends of my
limbs, spinning.

Dream #3.

Sally slouches in a doorway, her long fingers crushed into her
pockets. Past her are open fields, vacant lots. She's like the plot
of a movie. When she opens her mouth, I walk right through it.

Dream #4.

Last night it was the principal, I sat in a hard wooden chair in
his office.

Listen to my wise thoughts, said the principal.

I look close and breathe his language.

You think I am your high school principal but I am heh-heh God.
He said.

What is that like, I asked.

*Well, no one really knows what the law is, which means enforcing
the law is like Tag: if you're murdered, you're It.*

He was walking towards me, his hands red as crabs.

How do I know you're really God, I said.

*Because I keep my face in my office. Anyway, June's a shit.
Forget about June,* said the principal, his tiny teeth opening
and closing over flowers.

I know I'm awake when I can hear people talking.
Sally says, *I'm sorry Nick got two years.*
June says, *That's not true, he hasn't been sentenced yet.*

Sally floats a drowsy smile as she slumps against the car.
She says, *I'm glad to hear it, June.*

June stares. *Yeah right,* she says.

We pull closer. Watching the one on the ground. She's wearing
white shoes and yellow blouse, while another girl pounds her head
into the dirt. (A gang thing.
That was school.
Cause and effect are beautiful, one
tumbles
after
another down
the
stairs.)

I lean into Sally's face & I rasp *stuck up* & Sally looks amazed.
As she turns away I bring her head down hard against the trunk.

When I step back June kicks her in the gut. Sally grunts & spreads
like legs.

Then we get freaky, battering Sally's ribs with our soft shoes as Sally
slides down the car to the ground, wedging her under the rear tire.
Her head rolls as I kick her chest. She tries to twist under the car
& my lips foam with dirty language.

stuck upp FUK FUCKH yoo…

She softens like a beaten rug. She's grinning and moaning.
Tears bubble out of her cheeks.

Another whomp upside the jaw & she throws her arms up, shivers.

June grabs her ankles and drags her to the bushes, then we roll her
under the little quivering leaves.

The alley is empty except for the muddy red car, sagging on its haunches like an old dog. The car door opens with a whine & June slides in across the black seat, its ripped seams spreading open under her butt. *What are you doing,* I ask.

Get in.

What about my rats.

I don't give a fuck about your rats.

I don't want to go any place where I can't let my rats out.

June laughs soundlessly. I carry them down in a dishrag & gently lay it on the pavement. Trembling noses poke up out of the folds, then scurry towards the bushes, their tails dragging behind like skinny snakes.

We drive down our street. *What about Nick.*

The lawyer thinks he's gonna get time.

June takes the Dan Ryan towards Interstate 80, and the weedy city streets give way to suburban boulevards, lined with grass thick as a rug, fresh as television. Sally sprouted somewhere out here, where it's so white it glows. *And I was glad I did,* she said, so she didn't learn anything about racism.

Let's drop by Daddy's, June says. *Say long time, no see. Thought we'd pay you a little visit.*

She giggles. Daddy's in Arizona. I turn on the radio. *'Stop in the Name of Love.'* June and 2 friends practiced that song in the living room for the senior talent show, 3 white girls miming the Supremes. *Before You Break My Heart.*

I wonder how long it's going to take us to get to Daddy's.

I don't know, she says.

FETISH

(1) THE FEMALE BOYFRIEND

When I was twenty-two I was fucked over by a bisexual. Alternate Wednesdays and weekends, when her husband was on business trips. I liked it. Her name was Kate. As Kate stroked my lips she said,

An ideal surfaces. Interrogation is what's left after you spread your legs.

Kate was a successful journalist, and she wanted me to be a journalist too. She said I could break into the business with either sex or politics, but sex was easier because it required less analysis. She arranged for me to interview a prostitute named Becky. Kate said,

Whores accumulate privacy. What you do with it is your business.

Becky was a dyke. While I interviewed her she was washing her pickup truck. I didn't know what I wanted. Was there such a thing as a female boyfriend? So I asked Becky, "In the lesbian world, what is the difference between butch and femme." Becky said,

Femme means making pink the color of your interior, and then drinking a lot of fluid.

When Kate was out of town, I snuck out to a gay bar. It was all men until midnight, when a female boyfriend walked in, wearing a satin tux the color of blood. She approached me, and all my hairs grew wet while purses opened their tiny mouths next to my skin. She said, Touch me there. I said,

Which is the fold, the dot, the persuasion?

She answered, Accent the positive. So I did. But there must be something inside.

(2)

An ideal sniffs my rust.   An idea surfs my crust.

My mistress cuts & tucks one silicone 38D into my chest and then
      another, while I'm bound to our massive brass bed. Her kinky
      breath is soft as suede.

When I cry she tells me,
      The best titties are raised on the farm.

When I scream she says,
      Pain shreds & relaxes. You'll stumble over the real thing.
      Think of scrub brushes and the perfect ending.

When I sob in agony she comforts me,
      Later we'll take a tour of the castle.

My mistress is cruel. She's bright as breath.
      She whispers to me as she cuts,
      I'm a fan of the flesh — tits, stuffing, sweetmeats.
      I suck the juice from the roast, I'm a pig with a straw.

(3) BECKY

Kate asks me about my interview with the whore Becky. I told her
about the female boyfriend in the beautiful red tuxedo. Kate said,

I'm not prejudiced but I just like men better.

I relaxed. Relaxation is a cruel mistress. How many kinds of lace
do I have in my pocket? One, 2 kinds. The princess in the castle showed
me her precious garment: black panties knit from pubic hair. He plunged
his face into my hairs, the princess reported. Great, said my mistress,
We'll make a sex video from crushed lips & your razor.

When I'm scared I remember what the female boyfriend told me.
She said that sadomasochism makes theater from the alienated boy —
I mean body. I know that. I mean, We've always lived in the castle,
but true love is more subjective.

I think about the "lower stories" when I glimpse their fluids.
Vulva is bright noxious atmosphere, gleaming below. Don't you wish
you had a more stretchy wish, and a little privacy for your skin?
It's easier than thinking, & a few stripes cover the living room. One day
you'll believe your couch is your leg. Think about which is the female.
Remember, it's that or nothing — I mean a whipping.

Don't eat anything in this room. There are too many visuals.

NOTES TO THE POEMS

BABY

This piece was originally written for DRESS/CODE,
an exhibition at the San Francisco Arts Commission
Gallery which performed and examined codes of
gender identity. It was curated by Eliot Linwood.

FETISH

This piece originally appeared in the catalogue for
"Addressing Herself," an exhibition at The LAB
which addressed issues of female sexuality,
fetishism, self-representation, and transformation.
It was curated by Charles Gute, Minnette Lehmann,
Laura Brun, Michelle Rollman, and Zoey Kroll.

TITLES AVAILABLE FROM KELSEY ST. PRESS

DISTANCE WITHOUT DISTANCE
Barbara Einzig, prose
1994, 136pp., $10, ISBN 0-932716-34-2

THE VIEW THEY ARRANGE
Dale Going, poems
1994, 72 pp., $10, ISBN 0-932716-33-4

JUST WHISTLE   A VALENTINE
C. D. Wright, poems
Deborah Luster, photographs
1993, 64 pp., 6 photographs, $14,
ISBN 0-932716-32-6

SPHERICITY
Mei-mei Berssenbrugge, poems
Richard Tuttle, drawings
1993, 48 pp., 7 drawings, $14,
ISBN 0-932716-30-X
Limited signed edition with an original color
drawing, $200, ISBN 0-932716-31-8

ISLE
Rena Rosenwasser, text
Kate Delos, drawings
1992, 56 pp., six color drawings, $12.95,
ISBN 0-932716-28-8
Limited signed edition with an original color
drawing, $40, ISBN 0-932716-29-6

UNDER FLAG
Myung Mi Kim, poems
1991, 56 pp., $9, ISBN 0-932716-27-X

PECULIAR MOTIONS
Rosmarie Waldrop, poems
Jennifer Macdonald, s/kins
1990, 48 pp., 4 images on vellum, $9,
ISBN 0-932716-26-1
Limited signed edition
with artist's original print, $35

BED OF LISTS
Elizabeth Robinson, poems
1990, 48 pp., $8, ISBN 0-932716-25-3

LIKE ROADS
Laura Moriarty, poems
1990, 74 pp., $8, ISBN 0-932716-24-5

MUSICALITY
Barbara Guest, poems
June Felter, drawings
1988, letterpress, 48 pp.,
12 drawings, $9, ISBN 0-932716-23-7
Limited signed edition with
hand-colored cover, $35

SMALL SALVATIONS
Patricia Dienstfrey, poems
1987, letterpress, 32 pp., $8,
ISBN 0-932716-22-9
Limited signed edition with
handcolored cover, $35

SIMULACRA
Rena Rosenwasser, poems
Kate Delos, monoprints
1986, 49 pp., 14 color plates, $23,
ISBN 0-932716-21-0
Limited signed edition, clothbound
and sewn in signatures, $75

BAKE-FACE & OTHER
GUAVA STORIES
Opal Palmer Adisa, prose
1986, 116 pp., $7.50,
ISBN 0-932716-20-2

DESIRE$_1$
Thaisa Frank, prose
1982, 62 pp., $4.75,
ISBN 0-932716-15-6

GRAMMARS FOR JESS
& TWENTY-TWO CROPPED SETS
Marina La Palma, poems
1981, 56 pp., $4.50, ISBN 0-932716-16-4

POEM FROM A SINGLE PALLET
Fanny Howe, poems
1980, 32pp., $4.50,
ISBN 0-932716-10-5

DREAMS IN HARRISON
RAILROAD PARK
Nellie Wong, poems
1977, 48 pp., $6,
ISBN 0-932716-14-8